Humanity First!
Towards an Ethical Civilisation

The program of the New History Association 2021

Publisher: Uusi historia ry / New History Association
© Uusi historia ry 2021
ISBN 978-952-7352-10-6

Cover photo: A manifestation against racism in Helsinki, 24 September 2016.
© LEHTIKUVA / JARNO MELA
Cover and layout: Heli Santavuori

Humanity is now facing an era more turbulent than ever before. For the first time in human history, social upheavals and turmoil will occur almost simultaneously in all continents, in all different circumstances and political systems. (2003)

How does humanity know itself? All information relevant to the existence of humans must be re-evaluated.
  The time of reassessing all values, the great era of redefining all concepts has begun. (2016)

\- Matti Puolakka

Preface

The 2.5-million-year journey of the *Homo* family is coming to an end. It can end in two ways: either humanity will destroy itself or find ways to unite on the basis of its self-knowledge. Then our new history will continue in a global society, that is, in an ethical civilisation.

In this program bulletin, we present the most common perspectives on how humanity has come to this day, as well as some suggestions for the way forward.

That is our view – what is yours?

Helsinki, 13 June 2021

New History Association

The program of the New History Association is a summary of our views, based on the lifework of the Finnish philosopher Matti Puolakka. It is edited by Heli Santavuori with the help of other members of the Editorial Team.

Contents

Part III
Why Do We Need a New History?

Appendices

PART I
In Which Era Are We Living?

- The Crucial Question of Our Time
- The Past Era and the State of Ideological Debates
- The Change of the Era
- The Formation of a Global Society
- New Institutions of Global Society

PHOTO: Graffiti on the remains of the Berlin wall. Pxfuel.

The Crucial Question of Our Time

> *What is the reason for the self-destructiveness of the human species? This is the crucial question of our time.*

We are living in the era of the unification of humankind.

Humans, as a species, have become a unit of natural selection. It is a biological fact – no other animal species has the same quality. Humanity will survive or perish together.

Humanity is in danger of self-destruction. Nuclear weapons, climate change, and loss of biodiversity are all examples of the fact that humans are able to destroy the preconditions for human life on the planet. The threat of financial crises, recurrent pandemics, increasing inequality, and the ever-harshening social discourse are yet other problems for which we humans are to blame.

What is the reason for the self-destructiveness of the human species? This is the crucial question of our time. Finding an answer to this question is the most important ethical and intellectual challenge of our era. All other ideological speculations are subordinate to this problem. We should always go back to this question when we discuss current global problems.

The Swedish botanist and physician, Carl Linnaeus, placed our species in the genus *Homo* and named it *Homo sapiens* – wise humans. To his definition, Linnaeus added a remark: "Man, know thyself". His comment was intended for the entire human species. Hegel said the same thing categorically: the Delphic maxim, "know thyself" is directed to humankind, not only to individuals. In other words, humans become wise only when they know themself as a species.

Our sole survival strategy is the knowledge of human history and human nature.

Humankind can survive only by building its internal relationships on the basis of self-knowledge. Only in this way we can live in harmony with nature.

The most important goal of our program is to bring all humankind together to discuss and debate the basic teachings of our history.

The Past Era and the State of Ideological Debates

No traditional ideology has tried to synthesise the world views born in the past era – let alone link it with the new, epoch-making scientific findings on human origins or differences between humans and animals.

The socialistic world order and the global communist movement came to a dead end and a total collapse at the end of the last century.

Fifty years ago, none of the supporters of socialism could see this coming. Something happened that even those who now protest against "capitalism" and want to replace it with "socialism" cannot explain. None of those who strive to overthrow "capitalism" have made attempts to form a synthesis that takes the indisputably viable characteristics of a capitalist economic system into consideration but neither has any opponent of socialism been able to explain, in scientific terms, the collapse of all forms of socialism.

The "end of history" view was an ideological and political conclusion drawn by the supporters of western democracy: liberal democracy had won for good, and it no longer had any inherent threats.

This conclusion implied that there was nothing positive to gain from the defeated ideology. The fact that millions of people all over the world once were ready to sacrifice their lives for socialist and communist ideals was not explained, or if it was, it was an anti-intellectual narrative of omnipotent leaders combined with a racist-style image of ordinary people as an easily manipulated mob.

The threat of humanity's self-destruction, reflected in the deepening crisis of democracy, recurrent financial crises, and climate catastrophes, has proven the concept of the "end of history" wrong.

Historical events of the last decades have shown all, even opposing ideologies, to be inadequate.

The ideologies inherited from the past era all rely, knowingly or unknowingly, on some kind of overall view concerning human history as a whole, which is why the recorded history should also be re-evaluated. As to prehistory, re-evaluation has become a necessity because of the new, epoch-making findings on human origins.

How do humans differ from animals? How does human society differ from flocks, herds or colonies of animals? What are the psychological reasons for wars? Is there something in common in the social development of prehistoric and historical times? When looking for answers to these questions, the basic views and concepts they are based on must be evaluated critically within every ideological current.

---

[1] The terms socialism and capitalism are often used as if they were universally defined. However, this is not the case, hence the use of quotation marks. Defining these terms will be one of the central topics in the discussion on the past era.

The Change of the Era

The information technology revolution is a much more profound turning point in world history than the preceding industrial revolutions. The IT revolution and the globalisation sped up by it have caused irreversible changes in our economic and technical basis as well as interactions between states and individuals.

Industrial revolutions divided societies into two opposing classes, with the middle class dissolving. Conversely, the IT revolution has increased the number of small enterprises and brought about development of new social middle layers. A new kind of start-up culture has arisen; the market economy has expanded into new areas.

In the following, we discuss the change of the era. First, we look at it from the perspective of the world economy, then from the perspective of nation-states. The reason for this order is that it is precisely the economic globalisation that has brought new challenges to the whole world. Our focus, however, is on democratic countries, because, in our opinion, democracy and the rule of law are the only possible starting points.

The State of the World Economy

The most significant politico-economic consequence of the IT revolution and globalisation is that speculative financial capital has gained a leading position in the world economy. Back in the 1950s and 1960s, industrial capital still ruled over financial capital. Banks were nationally owned, and they financed the national economy.

Today banks operate globally, and the biggest of them concentrate on speculation instead of financing the real economy. In recent years, the financial sector has grown much faster than the real economy.

For major international banks, it is almost impossible to know if they are financially sound or not. It is difficult to estimate the value of various investment products or even the value of government bonds. A given value is also likely to change quickly according to the economic or political situation.

In short: banks do not know their balances, and supervisory authorities are as ignorant. Therefore, we can rightly ask if banking in today's world is, as such, on an illegal basis.

Speculative financial capital has gained a grip on the political leadership of many countries. Whenever there is a financial crisis, the banks are rescued. Governments have been forced to take the risk-taking of the biggest speculators upon themselves.

It is true that also in more stable democracies, speculative financial capital compromises the rule of law. On the oth-

> *Banks do not know their balances, and supervisory authorities are as ignorant. Therefore, we can rightly ask if banking in today's world is, as such, on an illegal basis.*

er hand, speculative financial capital depends on the rule of law to function and realise its profits.

Ever since the financial crisis of 2008, the world economy has increasingly relied on the unorthodox monetary politics of central banks: zero-interest rates, buying of sovereign bonds, aid to banks, and so on. Investors have profited more than the real economy. The situation has not changed during the pandemic. Exceptional circumstances have become the "new normal" in the world economy. Nobody knows for sure how this "new normal" works in the long term.

Neoliberalism has been the dominant trend in economics and economic policy since the 1980s. But now the time of its dominance seems to be over. There are growing demands that global social and ecological problems should be taken into account in economic thinking, economic policy, as well as in banking and business.

Democracy in a Crisis

After the Second World War, imperialistic states based on a democratic market economy responded to the challenge set by the socialist world order and the national labour movement: the principle of legality grew stronger, civil rights increased, and social security improved. All this resulted in an unprecedented rise in the standard of living.

Democratic market economy and the rule of law are prerequisites for social reforms. Democracy, it is widely acknowledged, is in crisis. Firstly, it is a crisis of legality[1]. Secondly, it is a crisis of political debate. Both are underpinned by the profound changes in the structures of society.

The Legality Crisis

Globalisation, accelerated by the information technology revolution, has set totally new challenges to traditional democracies.

After the cold war, it was widely believed that liberal democracy had won for good. The rule of law, as a necessary

---

[1] The contradiction between the principle of legality and the tendency to lawlessness has been the most important conflict during the history of the democratic market economy. In these times, that conflict has escalated even further.

part of a democratic form of government, was disregarded. This was clearly seen in the speed with which privatisation was carried out in the former Soviet Union and the countries in its sphere of influence, with the help of western advisors, at a time when legislation was still taking its baby steps and when there was no guarantee for the rule of law.

The European Union, in its present form, was also founded according to this trend: the rule of law was detached from the EU Treaties and other legislation as a separate "value". The Treaties did not provide for encompassing judicial review of the actions of EU authorities. The EU officials lack criminal accountability in cases where they violate the Treaties. In the context of the EU's eastward enlargement, there was no investigation on the actual implementation of the rule of law in the candidate countries.[1] This was the case, even though the rule of law was one of the conditions set by the EU, not only for membership, but also for the beginning of membership negotiations. Consequently, the EU has few tools to deal with its "illiberal" members today.

The influence of speculative financial capital is clearly seen in the crisis of legality in the USA. A glaring example of this – and probably the one that angered people the most – is the fact that none of the bank executives who caused the financial crisis in 2008 were prosecuted.

Citizens' trust in the US political system has downright collapsed. The whole society, including the media, legal system, and even actions taken against the pandemic, has become polarised and politicised. The changing of the president is not enough to solve the legality crisis; profound changes in the system of government are needed.

The democratic system has not been able to rise to the challenge issued by the speculative financial capital. This has increased dissatisfaction with democracy. Various kinds of demagogic and even openly fascist movements have gained popularity in constitutional states. There are fewer and fewer genuinely democratic countries.

However, history has shown that the model of liberal democracy is capable of renewing itself. It is still the ideal of enlightened people and protest movements in totalitarian countries.

Crisis of the Social Debate

Freedom of opinion is the foundation of all human rights - and a guarantee for their preservation.

The United Nations declaration of human rights states:

"Everyone has the right to freedom of opinion and expression; this right includes freedom to hold opinions without interference and to seek, receive and impart information and ideas through any media and regardless of frontiers."[2]

---

[1] We have made a thorough study on the membership negotiations with Estonia. The EU Commission's country report ignored many judicial scandals connected with privatisation. The legality of the judgments was not investigated. The same pattern was followed for all the other new member countries. Thus, it was by pure luck or coincidence which countries improved and which reverted in terms of the rule of law.

[2] Article 19 of the UN Universal Declaration of Human Rights.

Unfounded labelling of public figures is to deny them their freedom of opinion.

Unfounded labelling of public figures is to deny them their freedom of opinion. They are prevented from "expressing their opinion without interference" and from "imparting information". At the same time, the general public is prevented from "seeking and receiving" information through all sources.

Internet and social media have given individuals entirely new ways to influence the social debate. However, social media has also brought about new forms of persecution, hate speech and smear campaigns.

Widespread conspiracy theories weaken our trust in institutions and threaten social stability. The latest example of the danger of these theories was seen in January 2021 in the United States. As disinformation and bald-faced lies became part of the mainstream, they finally led to a violent attack on the US Congress. The threat of violence against legislators, law-abiding election officials, and representatives of media is still very real, and not just in the US.

Hostile foreign disinformation campaigns also hurt national sovereignty.

Problems concerning debate-culture and knowledge are a new kind of challenge as well to individuals and communities as to states and international organisations. Reform of the education system is essential for the saving of democracy. (See part I, p. 24).

Cultural Globalisation

Economic and political globalisation began in the 1980s. Cultural globalisation, however, had already begun after the second world war, especially in the western countries and spread from there all over the planet, in different forms over time and place.

Cultural globalisation included many different types of phenomena, e.g., existentialism in philosophy; black roots music and civil rights movement in the United States; rock culture since the 1950s; and hippies and feminists in the 1960s and 1970s. All these movements were part of a new cultural awakening. The significance of these phenomena is in no way diminished by the fact that intuitive movements, especially during times of big changes, can cause many kinds of unwanted side-effects.

The new cultural movement was especially concerned with lifestyle issues, existential problems, and awareness. In this respect, its influence prevails. If we want to create a philosophy of history that can meet the challenges of our times, we need to study the questions put forward by the western lifestyle and culture rebellions as an important part of the overall view.

Basic Communities, Social Alienation, and Identity Politics

The IT revolution and economic globalisation have caused radical changes also in our communities. Some basic level social structures (e.g., neighbourhoods, work communities, extended families and, increasingly, nuclear families) are coming apart. This is a general trend that naturally varies from one area to another.

In developed industrial countries, alienation[1] has become the most important and entirely new kind of social problem. Economic misery in countries with a high standard of living is very different from what it was, for example, during the first industrial revolution. But the higher standard of living and better social security have not necessarily resulted in better mental well-being. Fundamental questions of humanity, human relations and lifestyles are also important to people with an adequate standard of living.

Identity politics have lately replaced traditional ideological dividing lines: political groups are formed around race, sex, ethnicity, sexuality, etc. Defending the rights of minorities is, of course, part of a functioning democracy. At the same time, though, identity politics has added to the natural human spirit of "us against them". This results from the impasse of ideas inherited from the past era and the disintegration of basic social structures.

Thanks to the internet, it is now possible to create new kinds of communities and networks. However, this is just a possibility. The Internet has also provided a platform of networking for different types of violent marginal groups. No technological application alone can solve the basic problems of human existence.

In today's world, democracy cannot be defended with traditional politics alone. It is necessary to build, consciously, new kinds of human communities. Whatever their form and shape, they can only be founded on an open and honest social debate and study, encompassing the whole path of humanity.

---

[1] We use the term "alienation" here as a descriptive, not an exact concept.

The Formation of a Global Society

All human organisations that have existed so far – whether herds, tribes, or states – have been hostile to other respective organisations. The same is true even today - countries regard each other as potential enemies; that is why they have armies.

Global society does not have any external enemies, and it is not directed against any other human society or state. That is why global society is not a state at all in the traditional sense of the word. This is the most important vision to remember when discussing the future global society.

It will take many generations to form a global society. However, it is already possible to sketch its general features, even though it is impossible to say anything definitive about the details yet.

The following short presentation on the basic elements of global society is based, on the one hand, on a philosophical summary of the experiences of history and, on the other hand, on those future-related features that are already visible today.

The Basics Elements of Global Society

Global society has its roots deep in the democratic rule of law and in the development of international law.

The basic elements of global society are:

(1) Central authority is made up of international institutions, such as the United Nations with its sub-organisations, international criminal courts, and economic organisations. Eventually, these institutions will become democratic. The process is slow and complicated but inevitable.

(2) Econopolitical interest groups consist of independent nation-states within which political parties and other interest groups struggle over the distribution of income and power. In a constitutional state, this fight is regulated by laws.

(3) At the civic level, the most important new feature is the emergence of an ethical civil society. Networks of ethical citizens are the key element in the global society, the driving force of its development.

Central Authority

The central authority is not a political body. It functions as an impartial public servant and mediates conflicts between states and international econopolitical interest groups.

States and Political Parties

The global society is not a state. But the nation-states remain. They do not disappear in a global society.

Essence of State

All types of states in history, regardless of their social system, have the following three characteristics:

(1) States pursue their interests (as their leaders see them), against other states, if necessary. That is their *raison d'être*, the justification and reason for their existence. They do not seek and cannot seek to defend the overall interests of humanity. If they do, they do it only sporadically, at best.

Ultimately, states exist to wage war, either a war of conquest or a (just) defensive war.

(2) Political parties within states promote the goals of their interest groups. That is their *raison d'être*. From the perspective of humankind's overall interest, disputes between political parties are generally irrational, even when they pursue their own interests rationally.

Political authorities, however, have a tendency, characteristic of human nature, to obtain special rights and form elite groups which, given the occasion, turn against the rest of society and also against their own interest groups. Hiding facts and evading, even breaking, the law is part of the state leadership's nature, even in democratic states governed by the rule of law.

(3) The state mediates conflicts between interest groups. With the help of its institutions, especially its monopoly on violence, a state can dominate oppressed groups but also maintain peace and harmony in society.

A Change Is Taking Place in the Nature of States

The fate of humankind is in the hands of governments and the political parties that lead them This is a fact, despite the emergence of a global society. On the other hand, globalisation is changing the nature of states.

(1) In the era of the IT revolution, traditional imperialism has changed into financial imperialism. The age of conquest wars launched by the great powers in violation of international law is coming to an end or has already ended. This is a historic step forward.

> *Global society does not have any external enemies, and it is not directed against any other human society or state. That is why global society is not a state at all in the traditional sense of the word. This is the most important vision to remember when discussing the future global society.*

Financial imperialism means, first of all, politics with which great powers promote the interests of the speculative financial capital of their own country. However, a new phenomenon is that speculative financial capital has become a global operator, independent of all states, exploiting national property and tax revenues in all states, even in traditional imperialistic countries.

Although financial imperialism often operates above the law or against it, it does need legal protection to function and realise its profits.

(2) Economic globalisation coerces nations to respect the international agreements they have made, and restrains them from military attacks.

(3) Stronger international law forces nations to abide by it and limit their cooperation with countries that go against it. An important example of this is that violations of human rights are no longer considered solely internal affairs of states.

(4) International law can only be based on the sovereignty of states. As international law grows stronger, the sovereignty of states also becomes more secure.

(5) The threat of humanity's self-destruction forces states to think more globally in their decision-making.

(6) Thanks to the Internet and social media, citizens have more influence, both nationally and internationally. An enlightened public opinion can push states into making decisions that are necessary for the survival of humankind.

The history of the last hundred years shows that democratic countries are capable of renewing themselves. The specific features of this era, as described above, also imply that democratic states governed by the rule of law are losing their imperialistic nature. This is the most profound political change taking place in today's world.

However, it does not mean that there will be no more wars. It does, however, mean that future wars will be more local, and the long-reaching vision of a world without wars has become a realistic possibility.

Ethical Civil Society

The most important new feature in world history is the birth of ethical civil society. It forms a counterbalance to traditional political activity. It creates a sophisticated public opinion that forces political parties to change their views and will, little by little, change the nature of the state.

Ethical civil society can emerge only in the present time, in an era of human unification.

One of the most important social impacts of the IT revolution is that people are given new ways to have a global influence on both personal issues and issues that concern "the whole world". In addition to governments and parties, networks of communication created by ethical citizens are operating at global, national, and local levels.

With the term "ethical" we mean a sense of justice that is an end in itself. At the societal level, it means defending the human rights of all the citizens in the world and placing the interests of humankind as a whole before the interests of any interest group.

Traditional civic organisations are usually created around a specific cause, even if they have several goals. In this respect, also, civic organisations are interest groups. They do not represent ethical civil society in the sense we define the term.

At the beginning of the 21st century, as the internet grew, many groups advocating change tried to create a "network

> *Global problems are common to all. The debate must be open to all legal currents of opinions.*

of networks" or a "forum of forums". These attempts have inspired millions of people worldwide, but none of them has really succeeded in the original goal.

Here is a summary of our critique of these attempts:

(1) History does not begin with us. The starting point for the discussion must not only be the experiences of the past era, but also the whole human path and our common knowledge of the differences between humans and animals.

(2) Global problems are common to all. The debate must be open to all legal currents of opinions.

(3) Global ethical civil society can be built on debate only. Actions with no ethical or intellectual foundation will lead us astray and, at worst, create new grievances.

In Part II, we present practical suggestions on how an ethical civil society could be organised.

New Institutions of Global Society

Suppose our views on the nature of our era and the formation of global society go in the right direction. In that case, the following suggestions are both important and necessary. However, we want to point out that our proposal includes only general outlines. We can be more specific in our views only after criticism, discussion, and hands-on experience.

A Truth and Reconciliation Commission as a Permanent Institution

A global society can only be founded on the rule of law. Democracy in its present form cannot prevail if this principle is not fundamentally developed.

How can this crisis of democracy be solved politically? Here is our suggestion: every state governed by the rule of law (including unions of states like the EU) should have:

(1) a Truth and Reconciliation Commission as a permanent governmental organ and

(2) a Citizens' Truth Forum, run in cooperation with the truth commission. This truth forum should also have official status in society. The truth forum is presented in more detail in Part II (p. 35).

Collective Self-Deception

Collective self-deception, not open oppression, is the reason for the biggest social injustices in democratic states governed by the rule of law.

Truth commissions and truth forums deal with injustices that have become, or are to become, the norm. These injustices are always based on an official lie – a lie that is accepted, not only by politicians, but also by legal authorities, academic researchers, media, and, in the end, a large number of citizens, to their own advantage and often self-deceptively.

There is a tendency towards collective self-deception and illegalities based on it, even in the most democratic countries. A good example of this tendency is Finlandization .Another is the conspiracy theory, accepted by millions of Americans, of the "fraud" in the presidential elections in 2016 and 2020.

All the truth commissions so far have been temporary. They have often been founded during a transfer of power or a

 *Injustices that, due to collective self-deception, have become the norm are impossible to judge strictly according to the law*

change in the power structures. The most famous of these is the Truth and Reconciliation Commission of South Africa, founded in 1995 to deal with the events of the apartheid era. In democratic countries, however, truth commissions have concentrated on a specific issue, and they have not been linked to changes in power. Examples of these are the truth commissions in Canada and Norway, set up to investigate the treatment of indigenous people, and the one in Sweden, organised to investigate the activities of the country's security service.

Truth commissions have been significant historical steps forward in the processes of coming to terms with the past. But in democracies, a temporary body focused on specific issues is not enough to correct the injustices that have become norm.

To establish truth and reconciliation commissions as permanent institutions, changes in constitutional laws and, as far as the European Union is concerned, in EU Treaties, are needed. Naturally, the development and further definition of the idea of a truth commission is also necessary.

The Functions of the Truth Commission

Injustices that, due to collective self-deception, have become the norm are impossible to judge strictly according to the law – most political leaders and top government officials would be among the accused. It would also be hard to find such officials to deal with the illegalities who would not be obligated to recuse. The normal functioning of society would suffer, and there would be a threat of unrest.

The task of the truth commission would be to conduct a juridical investigation into the transgressions that have taken place. It could grant a general amnesty to those who confess to their crime or misconduct and are willing to participate in the investigation. Additionally, the commission might offer economic compensation to those who have been wronged.

A truth commission would make it easier for politicians, government officials, financial leaders, and opinion makers to admit their mistakes. It would dramatically decrease the confrontation in political debate. If governing powers are able to change, demagogy will lose its appeal. When the power of collective self-deception in society is acknowledged, there is no need for citizens to resort to conspiracy theories, at least not to the extent that they do today.

It is essential in our proposal to have a Citizens' Truth Forum which works together with the truth commission. The truth forum oversees the work of the truth commission. It also educates citizens at different levels of society to learn from history and to observe the world from the point of the overall interest of humankind. (See p. 35).

Ethical Citizens' University

Up to now, radical social changes have taken place in the modes of production and in political power structures. As humankind becomes unified, the most important changes take place in educational institutions.

University Reform Is Necessary

The most visible change in human development in the last five hundred years has been the triumphant march of natural sciences. And the march goes on.

Thanks to western universities and the successful research in natural sciences, humans have gained an enormous amount of knowledge on how to exploit nature. At the same time, however, scientific and technical progress has brought humanity to the brink of self-destruction.

Current academic institutions and educational systems have not succeeded in teaching humankind to control its own nature, that is to say, to organise its inner relations in a way that would help us engage in sustainable development and avoid self-destruction.

Universities all over the world are going through a change. In our opinion, what is needed, alongside the current universities, is a new kind of network between universities, university faculties, and research institutes. We call this network an ethical citizens' university. To implement this new forum, universities need to reform internally and renew their relationship with society.

A Synthesis of Liberal and Marxist Traditions

Our proposal is a summary based on the experience of the past era. For universities, this means a synthesis of the best qualities of the western university institution and the Marxist ideal of education.

Liberal tradition gives us the freedom to choose our research topics, freedom of expression, and the idea of seeking truth for its own sake. From Marxist tradition, we adopt the view, although reinterpreted, that some disciplines are ideological by nature (see p. 29), and the endeavour to form a holistic world view.

Some Basic Features of the Ethical University

Here we present our central views on teaching and studying social and human studies in ethical citizens' universities.

(1) Interdisciplinary study and research that tries to understand the whole path of humankind are needed.

(2) Philosophy must be in the lead. It is impossible to form a complete picture

of the human path without studying all the essential aspects of philosophy.

And on the other hand, the history of philosophy (more broadly, the history of ideas and culture) should be approached from a specific angle to see how the new knowledge on prehistoric, historical, and modern times confirm and explain some philosophical ideas – and overturn others.

(3) The ideological nature of research topics is recognised. Therefore, organising debates is the most important teaching method, and personal participation in debates is the most important learning method. By this, we do not mean the tradition familiar mainly from American universities, competitive debating. In the ethical university, the question is not of "who wins the debate" but "who argues most honestly".

(4) University reformation means, first of all, that the relationship between universities and political parties changes. Universities should organise free and open-to-all courses which bring universities and ideological and political movements closer together.

This kind of open courses in universities, adult education centres, and similar educational institutions all over the world will, in the future, form the heart of the global ethical civil society.

Gradually, the ultimate goal of the university reform pictured here will come true: a global citizens' university, supervised by the United Nations. Humankind will unite on the basis of self-knowledge.

PART II
What Is to Be Done?

- Principles of Discussion

- Human Path Debating Encyclopedia (DE)

- Citizens' Truth Forum

- A Great Discussion on the World Economy and Economics — Proposals for Banking Reform

- Guidelines for a Fair Debate

PHOTO: "Debate the Truth". Otto Toivainen paints a graffiti for the Truth Forum.
From a video by Erno Kaunela: https://newhistory.fi/citizens-truth-forum/

Principles of Discussion

The mission of ethical civic society – while defending and developing the rule of law – is to build, inside the existing society, new kind of ideological, political and economic foundations which can serve as building blocks for a new kind of societal system.

We will first introduce the principles of debate that are valid in all our proposals.

Ideologically Rational Debates

Discussion and research topics are ideological if they

(1) include opinions which, in some way or another, are dictated by interests – real or imaginary, conscious or unconscious, material or social-psychological – and if they

(2) reflect the debaters' view of the world and values of life.

Debate on ideological questions is always very emotional. Individuals tend to get irrational and arbitrary. This is also true with human relations and personal interactions. This is proven by political history, the history of ideas, and the greatest fiction.

This is a fact, and there is not much anyone can do about it.

Ideological rationalism means that the ideological nature of certain themes is accepted. Debaters recognise that they can become blinded by prejudice or by their unconscious ambitions. In this way, the debaters are open to criticism.

In an ideologically rational debate, not only opinions but attitudes are also discussed.

There is no such an impartial expert or fact-checker who could distinguish the "right" world views from the "wrong" ones. Not to mention that artificial intelligence could be used for this purpose.

A man in the street, a professor, a politician – they are all equal to express their opinion on ideological issues. This is the most profound argument for the universal right to vote.

Objectivity can be obtained only by placing different views side by side. In that way, debaters are forced to learn about the opposing arguments and the reasoning behind them, to see where they come from and if they are justified – even if we disagree with them.

When debaters accept their fallibility

and everybody's right to disagree, it may also help them get to know each other personally.

A fair debate is a precondition for ideological rationality. Slandering and distorting the opinions of the opponents means violating their freedom of opinion. In severe cases, it can be seen as a crime against human rights.

Ideological rationality is a challenge in personal life, on social media, as well as in public societal debate.

Whenever people evaluate themselves and each other, their conversation is ideological, no matter how personal or unpolitical it is. The difficulty is the choice between being rational or irrational: do you think before you speak or just say the first thing that comes to your mind?

The Most Important Human Right: the Right to Get Paid for Speaking the Truth

On the most general level, the emergence of an ethical civilisation is reflected in the following: "One must get paid, also and eventually above all, for a sense of justice, solidarity, and truthfulness." This a general principle, which can be developed into a number of practical applications.

Since people tend to behave irrationally and arbitrarily, we need to encourage them to adopt a civilised debating culture. However, this is not easy to do in a society or a group with conflicts of interests. Therefore, we need a principle according to which we credit people for their sense of justice.

True knowledge of the world – serious truth-seeking – means unmasking prevailing lies and going against collective self-deception. When persons seek the truth, for the common good and in defence of human rights, they become consciously exposed to other people's primitive reactions, slander, discrimination, and persecution.

The most important human right is the right to "seek the truth". Crediting people for their love of truth is the best way to protect and improve everybody's human rights. It is also a necessary step in stopping hate speech and malevolent information influence.

Economic activity is based more and more on the production of immaterial goods (services, applications, fruits of mental labour). It is impossible to measure the value of work mechanically anymore. Therefore, wages and other means of earning are to be re-thought in any case.

> *True knowledge of the world – serious truth-seeking – means unmasking prevailing lies and going against collective self-deception. When persons seek the truth, for the common good and in defence of human rights, they become consciously exposed to other people's primitive reactions, slander, discrimination, and persecution.*

If an ethical evaluation is not our conscious premise, then devious, ruthless, and power-lust activities are rewarded, as has already happened. Huge economic inequality and the impoverishment of middle-classes are signs of this phenomenon.

Power is the most important commodity. When people are rewarded for their sense of justice, power is distributed fairly.

Our proposal is a universal principle that can be applied in many ways. We use the word "pay" figuratively, of course. It can refer to various forms of reward, from reimbursements and scholarships to granting loans and creating new ways of earning.

The first step is to give material reward to those who are able to debate in an exemplarily fair and just manner. (See p. 33). Another application of the principle is the financial compensation that the Truth Commission grants to those who have suffered injustice due to their opinions. (p. 23). Additionally, the principle can be applied at the local level in giving out micro-loans. (p. 40).

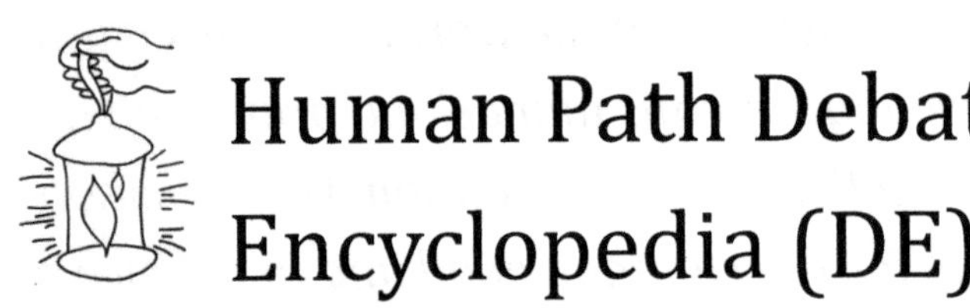

Human Path Debating Encyclopedia (DE)

The Human Path Debating Encyclopedia (DE) is a proposal to build a social media service suitable for ethical networking. It is intended as an instrument of humanity's self-knowledge for all people of the world, regardless of their worldview, nationality, religion, etc.

How to Organise the Debate

In the DE, users are encouraged to express their views as clearly as possible. Impartiality will be achieved by publishing as many writings on each topic as there are different views.

The aim is not to reach a consensus or to convince opponents. What is most important is to clarify the differences of opinion and to deepen one's own arguments by studying the objections.

All publications uploaded to the service can be shared. This way, also people untrained in writing or speaking can fully participate.

An essential new feature is this: anyone can assemble a debate panel from the site's publications and lead the resulting discussion. Moderating requires both an ethical attitude (supervision of a fair debate culture) and an intellectual effort (structuring the debate, dividing the theme into sub-themes, ensuring that the debaters stick to the point and take into account, and respond to, opponents' arguments).

But no one is obliged to start arguing against outright lies and nonsense. Panel leaders can exclude hecklers from their panels.

Especially in political controversies, debaters often do not discuss the same subject at all, just because they use concepts differently and do not even notice it. Therefore, the DE has a special section for definitions. The users of the DE can upload different definitions of concepts to the service. If there is a debate concerning, for example, "socialism" and "capitalism", the debaters ought to link to the definition they support.

Users can set up sites and groups to share speeches and writings published in the DE. In these pages, users can take their own "steps on the human path" – that is, to create publications with the help of, for example, a mind map-type application. In this way, each participant can use the service to build an independent and well-considered overall view of the world.

How Users Can Earn Money

Users get the ad revenues of their pages in the DE. The service encourages them to engage also in other kinds of economic activity, where they can utilise the social capital created by the service. Over time, the liveliest and most fruitful conversations will arise in sites where the debate is fair. In this way, the principle of "getting paid for truthfulness" will be realised.

The EU, other international organisations, states, universities and research institutes in different countries are welcome to launch the DE project. In our view, the global DE should aim to operate under the auspices of the United Nations or some of its sub-organisations.

The Central Theme: The Human Path

In these times, every serious and responsible party, NGO, scientific community and citizen has to reflect critically on the bases of their thinking; to re-create their worldview.

Each current of thought has to set themselves a challenge to learn from history in a new way. Every current and individual person has to ask the question "What is a human being?" in a new way.

For these reasons, the name of the Debating Encyclopedia is Human Path, and therefore it is also the main theme of discussions. The theme includes all philosophical, historical and social sciences, but also some fields classified mainly as natural sciences (ethology, paleoanthropology, archaeology, neurosciences, etc.) Furthermore, it includes the situation in one's own country and the present-day world, together with the prospects of humanity.

A top-down division of such a broad theme into sub-themes would, in our view, be wrong. The division in itself is a philosophical statement.

In the DE, each user or user group (scientific school, party, organisation, university professor, etc.) organises discussion on the main theme (or some aspect of it) in the way they want.

The initiators are to organise studies on the entity of the Puolakkaist philosophy of history in the DE, starting from the most general questions: What is everything? What is knowledge? What is justice? What is the human essence? What is human good and evil? We then proceed through the basic phases of human history to the present day and to the question "What is to be done?" At each stage, debate panels are set up in which our views are compared with other, divergent or opposing views and in which participation in the debate is open to all.

In the DE, people may also discuss any topic related to, for example, hobbies or other interests. Still, each participant should take a position on the main theme, even if only by sharing, reacting or commenting.

Guidelines for a Fair Debate

Ethical Guidelines

1. Do not distort your opponent's opinions. Do not slander.

2. Defend those whose opinions are distorted and who are slandered. Otherwise, you give your support to violations against another persons' freedom of opinion. Act to ensure that freedom of opinion and expression is truly equal to everyone.

3. Credit actively those who are capable of admitting their mistakes.

4. Credit actively your opponents if they deserve it either because of their exemplary debate culture or if there is something right or relevant in their statements.

5. Start from the fact that humans are capable of truthfulness, but as individuals and groups, they are, by nature, still inclined to subjectivism, irrationalism, and power games when their material, social psychological, etc. interests are in play. Start from the fact that it is easier for you to see this in your opponent than in yourself.

Intellectual Guidelines

1. Seek to look at each topic (a historical event, current political controversy, new scientific discovery, etc.) as a whole and in its context.

2. Avoid one-sidedness in evaluating your opponent's statements or opposing currents of opinions.

3. Try to know what you mean by the concepts you use and what your opponent means by them.

4. Stay on topic! The topics of debates ought to be delineated as precisely as possible. Otherwise, one demagogue may mislead the discussion quicker than ten honest debaters are able to rectify.

5. Try to distinguish the main issues from the side issues and the most important ones from the less important ones. In the Debating Encyclopedia, you can set up new panels to discuss subtopics and side issues.

6. Justify your claims. However, you cannot require the opponent to delve into a wealth of source material. Do not refer to sources to which others do not have access.

7. Remember that you don't have to convince your opponent. Once disagreements are clearly mapped, the discussion on the topic can be closed. It will remain in the service and can be returned to later. However, maybe you and your opponent have got to know each other during the debate and can set up cooperation regardless of your differences of opinion. An honest discussion may unite more than opposing views separate.

Citizens' Truth Forum

In Part I, we present a permanent Truth and Reconciliation Commission for every rule-of-law state as one solution to the crisis of democracy. (See p. 22) In connection with it – and to call for its establishment – a wide-ranging public debate is needed.

The Truth Forum is a platform for debate in which the search for truth is an end in itself. Issues are considered in the overall interest of humanity and evaluated from an ethical point of view.

The designation 'Truth Forum' is paradoxical – the overall interest of humanity, the "truth" in this sense, is sought on a "forum", through a debate open to all currents of opinion.

The Truth Forum requires citizens to commit to a civilised discussion culture and to learn the rules of fair debate. The idea of the Debating Encyclopedia is, in one respect, an application of the philosophy of justice to discussion culture.

Over time, the Truth Forum (or some part of it) can become a significant new channel of influence for citizens to be involved in "delivering justice".

The premise of the Forum is that humans can learn from their history. Established democracies are capable of renewal if they are challenged by enlightened public opinion.

The purpose of the Truth Forum discussions is to create public opinion that puts pressure on states, parties, international organisations, and companies to abide by laws and agreements and to make reasonable decisions for the overall benefit of humanity.

The Themes of the Truth Forum

The Truth Forum has four themes:

1. The Past Era

History does not begin with us. The most important new ideas in the history of philosophy have always been created by overturning the central views of the greatest thinkers of previous generations while upholding the core of those views in a new form.

How to look for the "truth" about the past era? We need to look at the opposing ideas that have had the greatest influence on the development of the era and find out what in them is sustainable and distinguish it from what is outdated and wrong. Which of the current problems are entirely new and cannot be answered by any past ideas? A new overall vision must be built on the basis of such an analysis.

Different schools of philosophy give a different weight to the concept of the past era. The period covered by the concept also varies. Such differences of opinion are among the debate topics on the Truth Forum.

By the concept "past era", we mean the period in which the worldviews of current ideologico-political trends, movements, and parties were formed.

We are looking for an answer to the question "How did we get here?" What was essential, for example, in the birth of capitalism? Why has it become the dominant economic system? What are the different stages in the development of capitalism, colonialism, and imperialism? What caused the rise and fall of socialism in the last century? How have the predictions made in the past era about the future of humankind come true?

The Past Era Truth Forum builds a bridge between learning from history and political influencing. It is a means of changing the world philosophically.

2. Recent History

The Recent History Forum assesses the most important events and related ideological and cultural policy debates in recent history from an ethical standpoint.

Who or which movements in recent history have gone against the current and criticised politics that has subsequently been proven wrong? Who have been able to predict future developments correctly? Who have been self-critical? Who have defended the rights of those discriminated against because of their opinions? Who have suffered because of their views and attitudes?

What kind of recognition should the state grant to such persons and organisations? What kind of financial compensation would be appropriate?

Even the most democratic states are rarely able to admit their mistakes and apologise to those who have been wronged, and even then, it usually happens many decades later.

When debating opinions relating to current politics, the debaters' ethical attitudes are generally not at the forefront. But when it comes to the most heated ideological debates and major events in recent history, the question is not just about who was ethical at the time. The discussion is primarily about who at the moment wants to acknowledge and compensate for injustices in recent history, and who wants to water down or belittle them, or to counter the debate on them in one way or another.

3. Juridical Forum

The role of the Juridical Truth Forum is to bring to light the illegalities of governments, political decision-makers and officials which have become, or are about to become, a custom in the country; in other words, issues that are neglected by the judicial authorities.

The principle of legality includes public proceedings, which is to ensure that citizens and the media can control the exercise of jurisdiction. In today's complex society, this has become difficult.

The designation 'Truth Forum' is paradoxical – the overall interest of humanity, the "truth" in this sense, is sought on a "forum", through a debate open to all currents of opinion.

We need a return to the basics, and at the same time, a new kind of civic education. Therefore, the Juridical Forum will also discuss the history of the philosophy of justice and the stages through which the current rule of law has evolved. Otherwise, exposing illegalities and finding the culprits may turn out disruptive.

The new forms of injustice, for which legislation should be reformed, are an important topic. The development of international law is also one of the themes of the Juridical Forum.

4. Human Nature

In "delivering justice", the starting point in some way is always how human nature is understood.

This Truth Forum asks: Is there a general, unchanging human nature? Can it be defined? What is the difference between humans and animals? What is human "good" and "evil"?

As for sciences, human nature as a theme falls within the scope of philosophical anthropology, theory of knowledge, moral philosophy, and psychology. Other relevant fields are cultural history, fiction, movies, religions, myths, etc.

Pertinent descriptions of human nature are collected from the literature. Together with personal life experiences, they form the basis for discussing the fundamental problems of being a human.

These discussions can be combined with the panels in the Human Path Debating Encyclopedia, that is, to the debate on human nature's historical formation.

A Great Discussion on the World Economy and Economics

> *The current stage of economic development, the dominant position of speculative financial capital in the world economy, cannot be explained on the basis of any existing economic theory. No economic theory alone is enough.*

Many economists rightly warned of the threat of a financial crisis before it came true in 2008. Yet even democratically elected parliaments failed to take these warnings properly into account and discuss ways to prevent the crisis. There was no discussion afterwards, either. Similarly, the risk of a pandemic was well known before 2019. Still, even in the middle of the COVID-19 pandemic, no one seriously questioned why preventive actions had not been taken.

Responsible politicians and social and economic scientists should launch a broad, simultaneously academic and popular, theoretical and practical public debate on banking and the role of the central banks.

The starting points for the discussion should be the obvious facts that, firstly, the current economic system is prone to financial crises, and secondly, in the cur-rent conditions, political decision-makers, directors of central banks, and banking supervisors are not able to prevent the crises.

We believe that it is impossible to have a serious debate on economic theory and economic policy unless it is extended to the history of capitalism (not just as an economic system but as a whole social system).

The collapse of all forms of socialism proves that a centrally planned economy, a one-party system, and the absence of the rule of law lead to totalitarianism and economic collapse. Despite this, the history of the democratic market economy is impossible to explain if experiences of the labour movement, the communist world movement, and socialism are ignored.

The golden age of capitalism - the Keynesian state-led market economy -

was, in a sense, a synthesis of the two systems. The labour movement played a key role, especially in the creation of the so-called Nordic welfare state.

We think the current stage of economic development, the dominant position of speculative financial capital in the world economy, cannot be explained on the basis of any existing economic theory. No economic theory alone is enough. We need a view on the entire history of humankind and, on that basis, a new

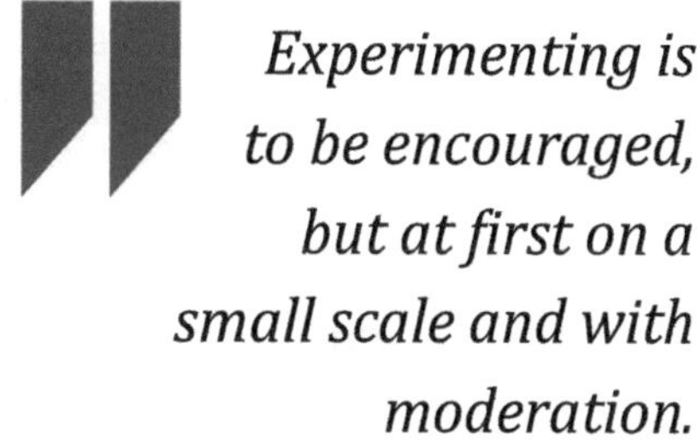

Experimenting is to be encouraged, but at first on a small scale and with moderation.

view on human essence and the development of society.

Proposals for Banking Reform

The world has entered a new era, and there is no going back to Keynesian economics as such. However, we think that western countries need some kind of revised version of the Keynesian ideas.

Banking that Invests in the Real Economy Should be Supported

Nowadays it is necessary to support banking activities that are non-speculative and concentrate on financing national industrial production and other economic processes. In this, it is important to pay attention also to environmental issues.

Local Banking Should be Supported

There are more and more areas that have lost their industrial and economic foundation due to globalisation. Their basic social structures are breaking up. These areas can be helped by setting up banks under the supervision of democratically elected local authorities. There are many examples of such banks all over the world.

At the same time, it is necessary to go back to the goals of the French Revolution, still visible on the map of the country's municipalities: basic political units should be relatively small. The creation of larger administrative units may be justified by reasonable arguments, but along with centralisation, efforts should be made to return to relatively small "village and township parliaments".

Experiments in Banking Should Be Encouraged

'Experiments in banking' means, for example, Islamic finance and socially controlled micro-loans in various forms. In what forms? This is a question that needs both discussion and experimentation.

Islamic banking[1] is known for the fact that there is no interest on loans granted by the bank. The bank and the customer share the risks as well as the wins. Hence, they are more equal than in the western banking system. The most speculative investments are forbidden in Islamic banking.

Socially controlled micro-loans are suitable for financing small businesses. We believe them to be effective in fighting back problems such as unemployment and social exclusion. When a bank grants micro-loans locally, the principle of rewarding for truthfulness can also be taken into use. (See p. 30).

The possibilities of currencies that are not dependent on states or central banks must be examined. Legislation must be developed so that they can be used legally and in a regulated way.

Experimenting is to be encouraged, but at first on a small scale and with moderation.

---

[1] Naturally, this is not an argument for the Sharia law. We focus here on some specific features of Islamic banking. Especially after the financial crisis in 2008, many Islamic banks have been opened in European countries, and their idea has been studied at western universities. One of these studies is a master's thesis completed at Aalto University (Finland) in 2012: https://aaltodoc.aalto.fi/bitstream/handle/123456789/2752/hse_ethesis_12737.pdf?sequence=1&isAllowed=y.

PART III
Why Do We Need a New History?

- The Evolutionary Phases of Human History

- Decentralisation of Power, or Hierarchical Fractionalism

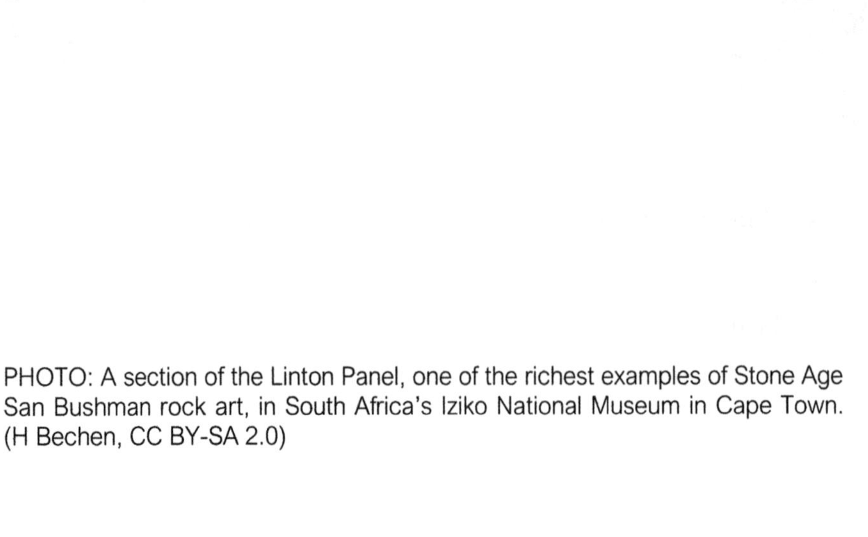

PHOTO: A section of the Linton Panel, one of the richest examples of Stone Age San Bushman rock art, in South Africa's Iziko National Museum in Cape Town. (H Bechen, CC BY-SA 2.0)

The Evolutionary Phases of Human History

The following is a summary of a forthcoming book series, in which the most important turning points in universal history are reviewed so that the main emphasis is on changes in the way of organisation. In those books, the Puolakkaist historico-philosophical view will also be presented and substantiated with empirical data, especially results in ethological, paleo-anthropological, archaeological and anthropological research. It is not possible to comment on them here; however the summary provides an overview of Puolakka's view of history.

Introduction

For philosophical history, the question of periodisation is essential. The division of periods must reflect the internal developmental logic of history.

Puolakka's philosophy of history is based on the one hand, the theory of societal evolution – that is, on the concepts of moral evolution, political evolution, and ethical evolution – and on the other hand, a definition of human society that is original and new.

In recent years and decades, many works have been published, in which the latest knowledge on prehistory is combined with an overall view of the history of humankind. Probably the best known of these are Yuval Noah Harari's *Sapiens – A Brief History of Humankind* and Jared Diamond's three-part series, in which he puts forward his vision of history. The most important work of the series, in our opinion, is *Guns, Germs and Steel*. William and J. R. McNeill's *The Human Web – A Bird´s-Eye View of World History* also evoked quite a lot of interest in its day. Common to all these works is the lack of a philosophy of history. They lack the background of a holistic vision of the history of philosophy, especially of the past era's ideological debates. The Marxist materialist conception of history has been adopted unnoticed and untold, and at the same time some of its fatal shortcomings have been accepted.

As a result, there is a huge confusion of concepts in the literature of the field. No scholar has been able to create a coherent picture. However, on individual issues, their work deserves great appreciation, of course.

The starting point of Puolakka's philosophy of history is a systematic critique of Marxism. On this basis, he has created a new synthesis especially on the ideas of the Enlightenment and Marxism. His view of the history of philosophy is Aristotelian-Hegelian-Marxist – drawing from all these currents, overturning them all.

Our Evolutionary Psychological Roots

Anatomically, humans descend from apes. However, biological evolution as such did not lead to the birth of the *Homo* genus. What was crucial was the change in the social organisation. The *Homo* genus has its roots in all animal species whose members influence their position in their community through reciprocal altruism.

When this kind of behaviour is socially inherited, it is a manifestation of animal moral evolution.

Moral evolution can be detected in at least some marine mammals (killer and humpback whales as well as bottlenose dolphins), birds (ravens, magpies, New Caledonian crows, grey parrots), canines (dholes and wild dogs), primates (chimpanzees, bonobos, gorillas, orangutans, capuchin monkeys and macaques) as well as vampire bats.

Bands of the *Homo* Genus

About 2.5 million years ago

A colder climate in Africa created savannas. In the new conditions, some hominid populations began to utilise carrion for food, as shown by the first stone tools suitable for cutting carcasses.

The hunter-gatherer economy was born. The individual band members' livelihood depended on the mutual division of labour between individuals and between groups of individuals.

The gathering of food through the division of labour required common rules and control. The distribution was done in a controlled manner at a shared encampment. Cheaters were punished. This was a new way of social organisation and therein laid the sprout of society.

"The spirit of laws" became the power keeping the band together. Therefore, in addition to the individual member, the band first became the primary unit of natural selection and finally the only one.

In terms of societal development, all representatives of the *Homo* genus, ca. 2.5 million to 60 000 years ago, belonged to the same species, including our anatomical equivalent, *Homo sapiens*, born at least approximately 200 000 years ago. Contrary to literature in general, we call all these species "ape-men".

Organisational development and better nutrition also contributed to biological evolution, e.g., by increasing the brain's size, which then furthered the leap in developing new tools.

This period of 2.5 million years saw the emergence of the gene pool regulating individual and group behaviour in humans. It includes both the blind lust for power and the ability to adapt to the rules that restrict it – the ability to overcome oneself.

Hunter-Gatherer Tribes

About 60 000 years ago

As the natural conditions worsened, some populations of *Homo sapiens* entered into permanent cooperation. Hunter-gatherer tribes were born. We call them proto-societies.

In a tribe, work and commodities were distributed inside basic units (bands), not between them. The basic units did not depend on each other for their daily livelihood. But all the members of the tribe were subject to the same rules.

The sense of justice was born, along with human consciousness. This is shown in the symbols, art, innovative technology and the ability to adapt to different conditions. Even earlier signs of these features have been found (e.g. in South Africa about 120 000 years ago). But compared to the evolution during the past 2.5 million years, the change was so dramatic and quick that no random gene mutation could bring it about.

The sense of justice separates humans from animals. It is, by its nature, a "judge's ethics", a willingness to think objectively – without prioritising one's own interest – in situations of intensely conflicting interests.

In a tribe, the rules were essentially human rights that protected the tribe members from each other. Humans needed society to protect them from their own nature. The tribe members could change their basic units (this was not possible in bands of ape-men). As a result, individual members of the tribe could unite to defend the values they considered important and build friend-ships and love relationships based on them. The concept of justice, the pre-condition of ethical intelligence, was born.

Within a tribe, an instrumental and an "end in itself" kind of sense of justice bound up.

The tribes were closed organisations. Other tribes were considered enemies. Against them, the tribal "us-spirit" was animalistic. Today, we know that there was more violence than previously thought, but no actual wars – going to war was not profitable. The evolution of society is a direct extension of biological evolution.

The tribe was a political organisation, settling conflicts of interest in society. Political evolution became the driving force of development.

Stateless Civilisations

About 10 000 years ago

In a civilisation, different modes of production were covered by the same administrative entity. Production became socially organised.

Civilisations began to emerge towards the end of the prehistoric era. Some groups of people settled permanently in areas where natural resources were particularly abundant. This was mainly, but not exclusively, related to the start of agriculture. It led to a permanent division of labour and trade with, e.g., farmers, cattle breeders, fishers, and hunter-gatherers. The process was long-term and complex and varied according to natural conditions.

The number of people covered by the same rules increased, as well as the size of the basic units. The division of labour expanded and diversified. The issue of commodity distribution became increasingly complex.

Within a hunter-gathering tribe, basic units were self-sufficient. In a civilisation, the livelihood essentially depended on the division of labour between basic units or even entire economic areas.

After the emergence of civilisations, the path of humanity divided in two. There were, of course, borderline cases between the basic forms, but at their most typical, the difference was clear:

1. Multi-tribal alliances were formed on the basis of lineages and clan ties, with one lineage and its chief rising to a dominant position. They were the first class societies and often very violent. We call them chiefdoms.[1] They were internally unstable and lacked administrative structures that would have allowed them to subject other areas to a permanent exploitative relationship. Warfare took the form of battles to control trade routes or farmland; sometimes it was road and sea piracy.

2. Egalitarian, peaceful civilisations, with some status differences and some signs of violence, but no evidence of actual exploitation and warfare. The best known are Çatalhöyük in Turkey, the Indus Valley Civilisation on the border between India and Pakistan, and Norte Chico (Caral) in Peru.

There were no written laws, even in the latter. But, for instance, the seals of the Indus Valley Culture, which were essential in marking private property, guaranteed peace in the society. Domestic units were relatively independent in managing their daily livelihood.

Peaceful civilisations seem to show Hegel was right when saying that private property is a condition of freedom.

Marxism, in turn, assumed that "early communism" – the lack of private ownership – would have been a prerequisite for justice, equality, and peace. That was not the case.[2]

However, peaceful civilisations disappeared in time. In them, society was not built for its own purpose but to exploit nature. Class societies became the mainstream of development. At first violent chiefdoms, later empire-building city-states. In them, ruling over others became an end in itself.

Unlike the tribes of hunter-gatherers, all civilisations were outward and open, seeking to expand. When internal relations were relatively egalitarian, expansion was peaceful. Class societies leaned on violence. Wars became part of human history.

State Societies

About 5 000 years ago

In a class society, human beings organised against other human beings, so that

---

[1] The concept of "chiefdom" is debated, for good reason. At the end of prehistory, a great variation of civilisations and social formations emerged. We think the classification of them from a point of view other than violence and relative equality is not worthwhile when drawing the overall picture.

[2] In the times of Marx and Engels, it was not known that there had existed high cultures – large networks of city-states – that were not violent and where there were no slaves.

ruling people became an end in itself. This was manifested in the first administration based on written laws in Sumer, where the first militaristic city-states also arose. The exercise of power became the most important work, the division of labour related to it became the most important division of labour, and power became the number one commodity. The utilisation of nature became subordinate to the building of society.

States are class societies where the rules that govern everyone are not based on tradition and custom but on written laws. Instead of kinship ties, a separate class of officials and a professional army were created to enforce them.

City-states emerged independently in only a few regions around the world. They were warlike organisations of exploitation and oppression.

Thanks to the new rule based on law and literacy, they could subdue foreign territories, nations, and countries relatively permanently. Although empires rose and fell, the state structure spread almost over the whole world during recorded history.

When city-states arose, humans became the greatest enemy of humanity. As a reaction to it, an ethical tendency arose, an aspiration for social justice.

The state societies also launched an unprecedented development of science, technology, and culture. It was fuelled by the struggle between opposing tendencies, which took place not only between different classes and layers of society but also within them.

Important milestones in historical times have been, for example, the following:

The birth of philosophy in ancient Athens. Philosophy – the search for truth as an end in itself – was a significant turning point in humanity's self-knowledge. It laid the foundation for a later scientific revolution. The debate over righteousness in ancient Athens is still one of the essential building blocks of a scientific view of human nature.

The birth of the modern world. During the Middle Ages, Western Europe lagged far behind, e.g. from China`s high culture. However, the lack of a strong central authority allowed the development of independent local communities. Since the 12th century, especially in the Italian city-states, a democratic and imperialistic market economy (so-called capitalism) was born. It launched an unprecedented but, at the same time, very contradictory development.

Production for the market required democracy and the rule of law within the ruling class. That is what separated the modern world from earlier class societies. The expansion of trade also led to the creation of international law based on the sovereignty of states. The Enlightenment ideas against the church's authority, the doctrine of separation of powers, and the idea of equal human rights were born.

Industrial revolutions initially led to working days of up to 16 hours on hunger wages, child labour, etc. The imperialist states carried out ruthless oppression in their colonies until their independence.

Under the conditions of the modern world, most of the population has increasingly had the opportunity to fight for democratic rights and equality before the law against economic exploitation and ideologico-political oppression. In all class societies, political activity defending justice always has an ethical aspect.

The past era and Marxism. The rise and fall of the global socialist system and the communist world movement was the most significant event of the era. When evaluating it, one must consider what it was created against, i.e. the developmental stages of the so-called capitalism from colonialism to neo-colonialism and world wars.

The democratic market economy and the rule of law have proven to be the only sustainable foundation on which to build. On the other hand, without summarising the experiences of the past era and without a preserving negation (in a Hegelian sense) of Marxism, it is not possible to create a new historico-philosophical view of the path and future of humanity.

The turn of the era. Speculative financial capital has become a global power. It includes forces that threaten the democratic structures of states. On the other hand, the information technology revolution offers entirely new opportunities for every member of the human species to participate in the decision-making of their own lives and of humanity as a whole. Material conditions for the ultimate, psychological liberation of a human being have arisen.

Throughout history, opposing tendencies for self-destruction and self-knowledge, lawlessness and legality, and war and peace have existed within the same administrative entity. Both tendencies have become stronger, but the tendency for self-destruction still dominates.

The development towards the unification of the human species began in state societies. But the reason and purpose for the existence of states is to defend their interests against other states – ultimately, war. Humanity can only become united when there is a profound change in the nature of states.

Global Society

Modernity and future

In a global society, humanity enters the path of ethical evolution. Its fundamental principles are the basic lessons of the history of humankind:

(1) Decentralisation of ideological, political, and economic power.

(2) One must get paid, also and eventually above all, for truthfulness, solidarity, and a sense of justice.

Global society is presented in more detail in part I, p. 18. About decentralisation of power, see p. 49.

Decentralisation of Power, or Hierarchical Fractionalism

We use the new concept of hierarchical fractionalism to describe the way in which a viable human society is organised. According to this view, "hierarchy" is to be understood essentially as an instrument; and fractionalism as an end in itself, a basic purpose: the most important task of "leadership" is to ensure that power is decentralised to a basic level so that basic units can maintain their independence.

Human society, just like any single human community, cannot be organised without some kind of hierarchy or centralised leadership. The importance of centralised administration and tiered power structures is emphasised if the community is any broader or its tasks more demanding.

However, human communities are also characterised by their individuals' intellectual and moral independence. Human communities always tend to divide into freely operating subdivisions that are independent of the centre and can decide on their own matters.

Dialectically, the more that global power structures are being formed as humanity becomes more united, the more important it is to maintain the ideologico-political independence of the lower levels (nation-states, and inside of them, local levels and basic communities).

This kind of organisation describes well, for example, hunter-gatherer tribes or peaceful pre-historical civilisations. Hierarchical fractionalism is also the form of organisation for the global society of the future. The dismantling of class societies begins with the decentralisation of power.

As social classes were formed, the basic human units lost their economic, political, and ideological independence. This was actualised very dramatically, for example, in Mesopotamia when the first empire-building city-states were formed. That is when the individual's alienation from oneself, one's work, and from society began. The same development continued both in capitalist societies after the industrial revolution and in socialist societies, where the major means of production were socialised.

Under the circumstances of the information technology revolution, individuals are drawn even more fiercely from their mental roots. Basic human communities established on locality, family relationships, and industries are losing their meaning and, at the same time, losing the last opportunity to decide on their own matters. The change is, evidently, irreversible. But the IT revolution provides whole new kinds of influencing options for creating new types of basic human communities.

Basic Human Communities

People can never truly escape their biology. Therefore, every person ultimately wants to live within a circle of acquaintances, where roughly everyone knows each other and can view and value each other as holistic personalities.

People create themselves both as individuals, and as a species. Human individuals want to decide on their own matters. The most important thing for individuals is their relationships with other people.

In human communities, the struggle for power is a struggle for "recognition". Individuals can pursue ethical authority by approaching conflicts of interest deliberately and objectively or by creating false self-images and gaining superiority over their fellow human beings through power play, slandering, and scheming. Human nature has the ability for both. Individuals always struggle between those two attitudes, both in societal life and in their personal daily lives.

Human individuals manifest their personalities best when they can "deliver justice" in a personal circle of acquaintances.

Feelings of benevolence, sympathy, and antipathy are (self-)critically assessed when they are related to the requirements of objective justice, commonly agreed values and rules.

People can be true to their nature when they can cultivate their basic characteristic, their sense of justice in personal contexts. That is real human growth.

The development of a new society is achieved both by traditional societal and political actions, as well as by constructing new types of basic human communities. The latter is more important.

The tendency to develop social classes is also characteristic of societal evolution. Resisting such a trend, that is, the oppression of one group by another, is the eternal task of humanity in all human societies on all planets throughout the universe.

APPENDICES

- About Matti Puolakka's Life Work

- What Do We Mean by the Philosophy of History?

- New History Association

PHOTO: John Lennon's Memorial wall in Prague. Paul Bowman, Flickr, Creative Commons.

Pertti Koskela

About Matti Puolakka's Lifework

We are undergoing the greatest upheaval in human history. The 2.5-million-year journey of the *Homo* family is coming to an end. Either humanity begins a new phase in its history, or it will perish. The threat of climate disaster, the loss of biodiversity and recurrent pandemics are the most obvious examples of this.

The Finnish philosopher Matti Puolakka (1947–2018) took it upon himself to summarise the human journey as a whole. Consequently, he also created a vision of a future global society, based on current, empirically observable phenomena.

In short, the global society is humankind organised on the basis of self-knowledge. How? – Part Two of our program presents some practical suggestions. Puolakka himself considered the

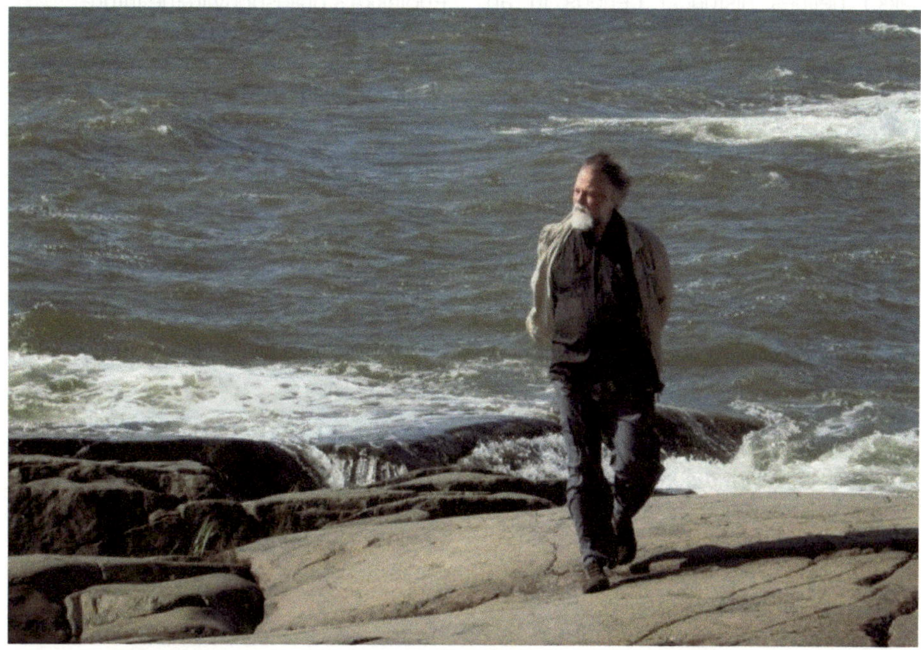

Matti walking by the seaside in Western Finland. PHOTO: New History Association.

idea of the Human Path Debating Encyclopedia and the Citizens' Truth Forum to be the culmination of his philosophy and the most important practical conclusion of it. The long-term goal is to bring the whole of humanity together to study and debate its history.

"...time apprehended in thoughts"

The philosophical universal history created by Puolakka, a unifying view of prehistory and history, is consistent, comprehensive and original.

The philosophy of history is the cornerstone of Puolakka's world outlook. His concept of history is teleological. It is based on his critique of Marxist dialectics from the 1970s onwards and on an original interpretation of Hegel's logic. Puolakka defines historical periods in an Aristotelian-Hegelian way bringing forth the internal development logic of history. There are laws in history – if history were merely a chaos of events, humans could not learn anything from it.

Puolakka offers a survival guide for humanity: the development of humanity's self-knowledge – the whole history of philosophy – must be combined with the actual, econopolitical history of the *Homo* family. The current era is an era of the unification of humankind.

Puolakka once said:

"Summaries of the whole journey of humankind are the most important knowledge for us on humans, society and the world in general. There is no other ultimate barrier against barba-rism. Kant called them universal histories."

Puolakka was, above all, a philosophical system builder. But at the same time, he was a consistent defender of freedom of discussion. No "ultimate truth" can ever be found. After their victory, philosophical systems divide into different, even opposing currents and eventually become overturned. This has always been the case in the history of ideas, as the historical fates of both Hegel and Marxism show, for example. As to Marxism, Puolakka emphasised since the end of the 1970s that lessons can be drawn on Marxism only if it is overturned as a system. If considered to be sufficient as a system, Marxism becomes a religion. This is the case with all philosophical systems when they become obsolete. The same will also happen with Puolakka's philosophy in the future.

Like all true philosophers, Puolakka saw as his mission "comprehend what is"; he was "a child of his time ". Puolakka's view is, again in Hegel's words, "its own time apprehended in thoughts ".[1]

It is possible for us to apprehend our time only by apprehending how it was born from within the past era. When Puolakka outlined the basic features of the global society, he did not come up with wishful ideas of "how it should be" but instead studied "how did we get here".

Three major sources of Puolakka's philosophy

Puolakka's worldview has three main sources:

---

[1] Hegel's Philosophy of Right, translated T.M. Knox, Oxford University Press, reprint 1981, p. 11

1. New scientific findings on prehistory, human origins, and the difference between humans and animals.

2. Phenomena related to the changing of the era: the rise and fall of socialism and the emergence of "red fascism" in socialist countries; the information technological revolution; globalisation and the rise of speculative financial capital; the founding of the EU and its chronic crisis; and the destructive human impact on our environment.

3. Personal life experiences. Puolakka saw that even people with high moral standards can fall into envy and bitterness towards a good friend. Even people who have worked admirably for some good cause can fall into a blind social-psychological power game within their circle of friends. Nonetheless, he never lost his fundamental trust in human potential.

Towards a New Overall View on Human History

Puolakka started out as a Marxist thinker, but early on, his views went far beyond the framework of Marxism.

In the late 1960s and early 1970s, he and his friends supported the rebellion movement in China, the so-called Cultural Revolution, which was designed to prevent bureaucratisation of China the way as had happened in the Soviet Union. But as early as in 1971, he began to criticise the Marxist moral-philosophical line, shared by all Marxist currents, which was the ideological basis for the extremities during the Cultural Revolution. The ideal – "absolute unselfishness" – led to self-denial, self-deception, and hypocrisy. Puolakka also criticised the view on human nature of the Cultural Revolution – especially the attitude toward opponents and those who supposedly had made mistakes.

He replaced the ideal of unselfishness with the principle of self-knowledge.

In 1982 he published a book called "The Crucial Question Is the Human Essence. The Crisis of Marxism, the Biggest Turn in World History and the Necessity of a New World Outlook".[1] With the failure of the Cultural Revolution in the background, it took the form of a systematic critique of the Maoist philosophy, but at the same time, it demonstrated the incoherence and inadequacy of all the central concepts of Marxism. – The greatest mistake of all different Marxian schools was to deny or downplay the significance of a universal human nature.

He then rejected the socialist project entirely, though admitting the enduring philosophical value of some Marxist views.

From the early 1990s, he dedicated his life to creating his own view of universal history – the grand narrative of this age. There is no greater task modern philosophers can set for themselves.

Because the view is new, he had to create new concepts or give established concepts more precise or more or less different content than before.

Puolakka was relatively unknown as a thinker during his lifetime, although his

---

[1] In Finnish: "Mikä ihminen on? Marxismin kriisi, maailmanhistorian suurin käänne ja uuden maailmankatsomuksen välttämättömyys", Osuuskunta Aurora 1982.

views were the subject of theses at Finnish universities.[1] His philosophical production is extensive, but he published very little during his life. Why?

A Man Who Knew too Much

Since the 1970s, he was subjected to a range of physical and psychological persecution, unique in the history of western democracies. He was a man who knew too much.

Firstly, in the 1970s and 1980s, he led research groups on Finlandization, the nature of the Soviet Union and its imperialist foreign policy. Critical research on the Soviet Union was practically forbidden in Finland at the time; there was none of it in Finnish universities. A law was proposed in Parliament to prohibit criticism of the Soviet Union – luckily, it did not get enough support.

Puolakka predicted, on analytical arguments, the collapse of the Soviet Union ten years before it happened, only to be met with scornful laughter. The influential circles in Finland never forgave Puolakka and his associates for telling the truth about Finlandization at a time when the entire Finnish political and cultural elite had given in to self-censorship.

Secondly, Puolakka saw and was able to explain all too well what was going on around him, for example, the Russian hybrid influence in Finland from the beginning of the 21st century. It intensified gradually, and as late as after the occupation of Crimea, the Finnish society has little by little woken up.

Thirdly, as early as at the turn of the millennium, during the eastern enlargement of the European Union, he saw the deepening legality crisis into which the Union was heading. This view was partly based on our own experience: we intended to establish a research centre in Estonia to organise studies and debates about the philosophy of history, the turn of the era, phenomena in the recent history of different countries, e.g., Finlandization. We hoped the University of Tartu would take the intellectual lead in the project. The idea was to combine the studies and debate with cultural activities and tourism. The project was destroyed with well-organised slander campaigns in both Finnish and Estonian media and finally with a Kafkaesque show trial and a juridical murder in Estonia. Despite all its progress, Estonia was notorious for numerous judicial scandals during the privatisation process between 1995 and 2004.

"I am not afraid to be philosophico-politically alone..."

In those difficult circumstances, Puolakka concentrated all his efforts on completing his philosophical overall vision.

---

[1] *Saarto, Ari*: "Dialectics as a doctrine of the unity of opposites. Examination of Matti Puolakka's view", master's thesis in theoretical philosophy, Helsinki University 1999. Prof. Ilkka Niiniluoto. (In Finnish); *Vainio, Timo*: "The collapse of communism from the perspective of Matti Puolakka's universal history", approved research plan at prof. Erkki Kouri's licentiate seminar, Helsinki University 2003. (In Finnish); *Vainio, Timo*: "Examination of the concept of work from the point of view of morality, dissertation in sociology", Tampere University 1987. Prof. Raimo Blom. (In Finnish).

Leo Tolstoy once wrote:

"To a lackey no man can be great, for a lackey has his own conception of greatness."[1]

In Finnish social media, press and literature, Puolakka has mainly been either ignored or exposed to slander, lies and misrepresentations. We will respond to them in due course. There is one striking feature to all of them: they ignore his life work and instead concentrate passionately to blacken his character. Those writings say a lot about their authors, but about Puolakka they only say that his greatness as a thinker and as a human being was and is incomprehensible to the "lackeys".

"No one is a prophet in their own land". Because of the peculiar recent history of Finland, the saying that has become folk wisdom suits Puolakka better than perhaps any other contemporary philosopher. We believe that Puolakka will first get the credit he deserves elsewhere than in Finland. So thought also Puolakka himself. He knew he had something important to say to humanity.

Matti Puolakka described his attitude in 2015:

"I'm free because I think about what is right and what is wrong. It is the main problem for me. That is why I live for humankind, not for myself. That is why I'm not afraid to set myself philosophico-politically alone – well, alone with my friends – against the rest of the world."

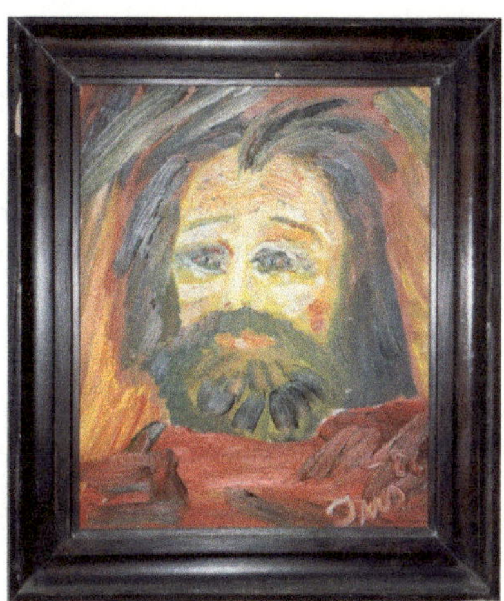

Matti Puolakka's portrait by Iris Keinänen.

---

[1] Tolstoy Leo, War and Peace, Book Fifteen, Chapter V.

What Do We Mean by the Philosophy of History?

The Encyclopædia Britannica presents the following definition:

> **"Philosophy of history**, the study either of the historical process and its development or of the methods used by historians to understand their material."[1]

By the philosophy of history, we mean the previous definition: the study of the historical process and its development. We also use it as a synonym for the term "universal history" created by Immanuel Kant.

All the great philosophers of history have presented the 'human path' in the following way:

1. They have explained the essential difference between humans and animals as briefly, succinctly and simply as possible.

2. They have summarised the basic phases of the development of humankind. In doing that, Occam's razor must be used: the presentation must be as short as possible. Everything unnecessary must be removed.

3. The present is an integral part of history. Thus, a philosophical presentation of universal history should outline, clarify, and sharpen the basic teachings of history. Only in this way it is possible to see the main trends of the future.

---

[1] https://www.britannica.com/topic/philosophy-of-history

Pia Länsman

New History Association

The New History Association was founded to support publishing, discussion and research based on the lifework of the Finnish philosopher Matti Puolakka (1947–2018). We believe that the significance of his philosophy will be epoch-making for disciplines that explore (pre)history, the history of philosophy, and humankind's survival strategies.

In his will, Matti left the editing and publishing rights of his entire literary and audio-visual heritage to our association and instructed us to set up a foundation to manage the publication of it as soon as financially possible.

Editing

Matti left behind a vast amount of material, mostly extempore dictations and half-finished edits – naturally all in Finnish. He didn't have a chance to finalise his writings, in particular the latest ones. He was looking for ideas and did not always bother to correct occasional slips or to finish his texts editorially.

His thoughts also evolved over the years; some perspectives and theses turned out to be erroneous while others deepened. For him, developing philosophy was thus a process of constant self-criticism and a rebuttal of his earlier views. Thus, he lived the transition from one era to another also on the level of thoughts.

In his summaries, he relied on extensive literature and research material of various disciplines. New findings on prehistory across the globe were important to him. But what matters the most are the conclusions he drew from them based on the philosophy of history and social philosophy. As he often said: "The first human is found by thinking, not by walking!" – Theorising based on research in the individual sciences is not enough to form an overall view of human history. We need a "philosophy of prehistory".

We were involved in discussions with Matti and edited his texts, but as a philosopher, he was a dissident in the deepest sense of the word. He revolutionised his own thinking and went against the current not only in society but also within his circle of friends. His views often arose when he had to confront his friends' attitudes, prejudices, scepticism, and even outright sabotage. These facts have been documented in numerous speeches and writings. In his circle of friends, he was always generous in giving credit to those who – in his opinion – contributed creatively to the development of ideas during discussions. He was conscientious in such matters.

We believe that this very significant and unbelievable story will be told, and future generations will study and wonder about it.

These are the premises for our editorial team to publish edits of the Puolakkaist philosophy of history and articles illustrating the concept of the Debating Encyclopedia from various angles – e.g. from the perspective of today's threats to the civilised debate culture. Democracy depends on how well these threats are repelled.

There are bound to be flaws in our edits. We hope they do not prevent the reader from discovering the originality, consistency and relevance of the views expressed. We hope for a lot of feedback, criticism and discussion on all the texts.

Publishing

A Proposal for a New History of Humankind

is a book series we will publish soon. In it, the Puolakkaist philosophy of history is presented by going through the latest empirical research on both prehistory and historical time. The article "The Evolutionary Phases of Human History" (p. 40) is a summary of the book series.

The first part will be published in English later this year. It covers the period from the birth of the *Homo* genus to the birth of human society and modern humans about 60 000 years ago.

Only Humans Have History – Thoughts of a Man Who Defined the Human Being

This book contains excerpts from Matti Puolakka's writings, messages and diaries. It gives an overall picture not only of Puolakka's philosophical lifework but also of him as a person and a friend and of his exceptional destiny as a Finnish dissident.

The quotations of Puolakka's writings

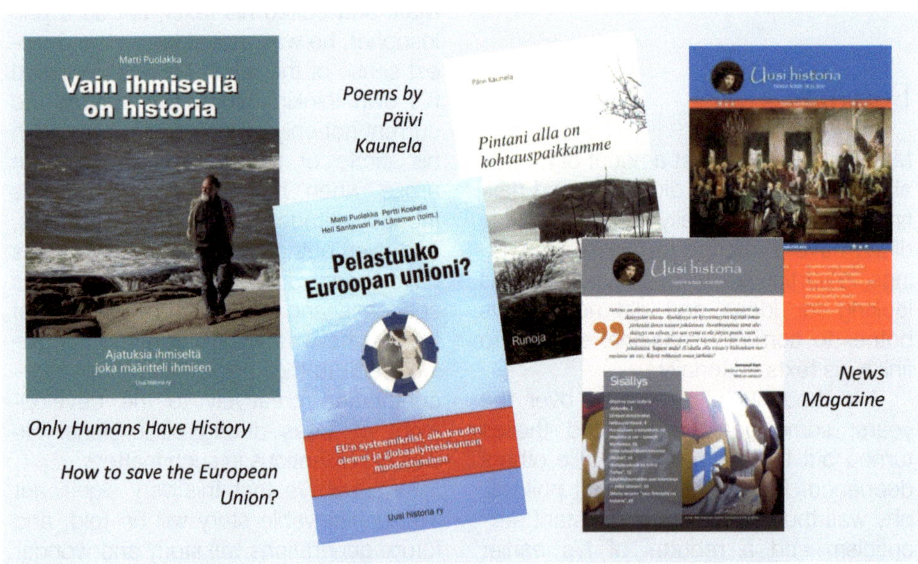

Only Humans Have History

How to save the European Union?

News Magazine

Some of the Association's publications in Finnish.

published on our English website are from this book. There are plans for an English translation.

Human Path Debating Encyclopedia (DE)

Matti considered the concepts of the Human Path Debating Encyclopedia (p. 32) and the Truth Forum (p. 35) to be the culmination of his life's work and its most important practical application. He hoped that the DE interface could be coded in time for him to publish his views in it, but it did not happen.

We are now looking for funding for the web design and coding of the DE. We plan to launch a crowdfunding campaign as soon as the most important texts on Matti's philosophy have been published in English. For now, if you consider that these ideas have value, not necessarily as ready-made answers, but as a vision and relevant questions, you can support our publishing work by purchasing this program bulletin or buying books or other products through our website.

Research Centre

The highest practical dream we have shared with Matti is a research centre to be run jointly with, e.g., universities and cultural organisations in different countries, following the principles of the Debating Encyclopedia in its discussion and research. Such an international centre would combine scientific and artistic creativity with start-up entrepreneurship, vacationing and leisure. Establishing the research centre is an integral part of our plans for the future.

Editorial Team

Pertti Koskela

**Chief Editor
Vice-President of the Association**

Pia Länsman

**Editor
President of the Association**

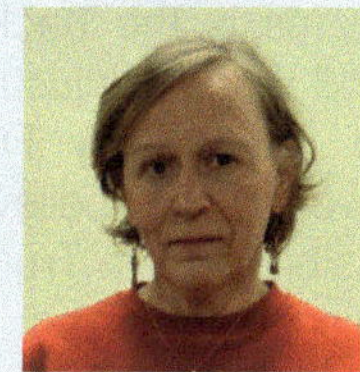

Heli Santavuori

**Editor, Design
Member of the Board**

Other Board Members

Päivi Kaunela – Research & Poetry
Sinikka Littu – Research & Cultural History
Reima Ukura – Research & Philosophy

The Story Behind the Ideas

An important part of the Puolakkaist philosophy is the idea of fiction that combines art and science: non-moralising reflections of one's own life experiences through a scientific definition of human nature. We believe that this could become a new genre in literature.

Many members of our association have been involved in ideologico-political movements and scientific research projects led by Matti since the 1970s and 1980s. Together we are working on his biography. We are also writing our own memoirs.

It is also the association's mission to tell – in both scientific and artistic form – the story of how these ideas were born. It forms is the background for our demand that the injustices in recent history and present-day Finland are rectified. However, we believe this will only be possible once a Truth Commission is established in Finland.

Activities

So far, we have been active on a small scale. Our research groups focus on philosophical topics and on recent Finnish history, the development of the EU, and world-historical trends in global politics and cultural history.

We have organised public events at the annual meetings of the Finnish Social Forum in Helsinki. Small-scale meetings are held regularly. In them, we often combine different forms of physical exercise or cultural content with philosophical discussions.

Contact

New History Association

Uusi historia ry
Reg nr: 2678671-8
Helsinki, Finland

Webpages

https://newhistory.fi (English)
https://humanpath.net (Finnish)

Email

editors@newhistory.fi
uusihistoria@humanpath.net

Donations

IBAN FI96 5721 1520 3352 53
BIC OKOYFIHH

Notes